THE USES OF
ADVERSITY

CARLFRED BRODERICK

WITH A FOREWORD BY EMILY WATTS

DESERET
BOOK

SALT LAKE CITY UTAH

Library of Congress Cataloging-in-Publication Data

Broderick, Carlfred Bartholomew.
    The uses of adversity / Carlfred Broderick ; with a foreword by Emily Watts.
       p. cm.
    ISBN-13: 978-1-59038-851-8 (hardbound : alk. paper)
    1. Suffering—Religious aspects—Church of Jesus Christ of Latter-day Saints. 2. Suffering—Religious aspects—Mormon Church. 3. Suffering. 4. Pain—Religious aspects—Church of Jesus Christ of Latter-day Saints. 5. Pain—Religious aspects—Mormon Church. 6. Pain—Psychological aspects. I. Title.
    BX8643.S93B76 2007
    248.8'6—dc22   2007043844

Printed in the United States of America
Worzalla Publishing, Co., Stevens Point, WI

10   9   8   7   6   5   4   3   2   1

Foreword

What do you say to a person in pain? What kind of answers are there for the truly hard questions of life, the imponderables, the times when every piece of counsel or word of comfort that comes to mind just seems hollow?

I've wrestled with those questions for years. And I know others have as well, because many of my friends have asked me, as a "book person," what reading I might recommend for someone who was undergoing a particularly soul-wrenching trial.

I never had quite the right answer, until the day a few years ago when I encountered Carlfred Broderick's incredible essay on the uses of adversity. First delivered as an address at a BYU Women's Conference, this insightful look at the pain inherent in our mortal experience changed my outlook forever. I have pondered it again and again. Over the years I have found myself sharing the stories with friends, using them in lessons, thinking of them when I felt I was floundering in my own (relatively minor) difficulties.

"The gospel of Jesus Christ is not insurance against pain," writes Dr. Broderick. "It is resource in event of pain, and when that pain comes . . . rejoice that you have resource to deal with your pain." He goes on to demonstrate the amazing resource that is available to all of us through the atonement

of Jesus Christ. And he does it with real-life examples of the hardest kinds of pain imaginable, from a mother who watches her family abandon the standards of the gospel to cases of abuse to the accidental death of a child.

Maybe I resonate with Dr. Broderick's approach because I'm a story person myself, and he makes his various points with true stories. Perhaps I am particularly swept away by his engaging writing style. But I think the real reason this work touches me so deeply is that it speaks the truth, the hard truth, about the way life is and illustrates the kind of faith we all ultimately have to find in order to get through it.

When there are no earthly answers, when our understanding is stretched beyond its limit, when mortality is simply too much for us, there is hope. As one

bereaved mother said, "I am content that God be God. I know he lives and loves us, that he is God. He's not unmindful of us. We do not suffer out of his view. I used to think we were safe from grief and pain here because of our faith. I know now that is not true, but we are safe in his love. We are protected in the most ultimate sense of all—we have a safe home forever. That is my witness."

It is also Carlfred Broderick's witness, a legacy he left behind when he died of cancer in July 1999 at the age of 67. It is my great joy that this "resource in event of pain" is once again being made available to help an even wider group of people. I have never read a finer treatment of the role adversity can play in the life of a person who understands the gospel of Jesus Christ.

EMILY WATTS

THE USES OF ADVERSITY

While I was serving as a stake president, I was once sitting on the stand at a combined meeting of the stake Primary board and stake Young Women's board where they were jointly inducting from the Primary into the Young Women's organization the eleven-year-old girls who that year had made the big step. They had a lovely program. It was one of those fantastic, beautiful presentations—a take-off on *The Wizard of Oz,* where Dorothy, an eleven-year-old girl, was coming down the yellow brick road together with the Tin

Woodman, the Cowardly Lion, and the Scarecrow. They were singing altered lyrics about the gospel. And Oz, which was one wall of the cultural hall, looked very much like the Los Angeles Temple. They really took off down that road. There were no weeds on that road; there were no Munchkins; there were no misplaced tiles; there was no Wicked Witch of the West. That was one antiseptic yellow brick road, and it was very, very clear that once they got to Oz, they had it made. It was all sewed up.

Following that beautiful presentation with all the snappy tunes and skipping and so on, came a sister who I swear was sent over from Hollywood central casting. (I do not believe she was in my stake; I never saw her before in my life.) She looked as if she had come right off the cover of a fashion magazine—every hair in place—with a

photogenic returned missionary husband who looked like he came out of central casting and two or three, or heaven knows how many, photogenic children, all of whom came out of central casting or Kleenex ads or whatever. She enthused over her temple marriage and how wonderful life was with her charming husband and her perfect children and promised that the young women too could look like her and have a husband like him and children like them if they would stick to the yellow brick road and live in Oz. It was a lovely, sort of tear-jerking, event.

After the event was nearly over, the stake Primary president, who was conducting, made a grave strategic error. She turned to me and, pro forma, said, "President Broderick, is there anything you would like to add to this lovely evening?"

I said, "Yes, there is," and I don't think

she has ever forgiven me. What I said was this: "Girls, this has been a beautiful program. I commend the gospel with all of its auxiliaries and the temple to you, but I do not want you to believe for one minute that if you keep all the commandments and live as close to the Lord as you can and do everything right and fight off the entire priests quorum one by one and wait chastely for your missionary to return and pay your tithing and attend your meetings, accept calls from the bishop, and have a temple marriage, I do not want you to believe that bad things will not happen to you. And when that happens, I do not want you to say that God was not true. Or to say, 'They promised me in Primary, they promised me when I was a Mia Maid, they promised me from the pulpit that if I were very, very good, I would be blessed. But the

boy I want doesn't know I exist, or the missionary I've waited for and kept chaste for so we both could go to the temple turned out to be a flake,' or far worse things than any of the above. Sad things—children who are sick or developmentally handicapped, husbands who are not faithful, illnesses that can cripple, or violence, betrayals, hurts, deaths, losses—when those things happen, do not say God is not keeping his promises to me. The gospel of Jesus Christ is not insurance against pain. It is resource in event of pain, and when that pain comes (and it will come because we came here on earth to have pain among other things), when it comes, rejoice that you have resource to deal with your pain."

Now, I do not want to suggest for a moment, nor do I believe, that God visits us with all that pain. I think that may occur in

The gospel of Jesus Christ

is not insurance against pain.

It is resource in event of pain.

individual cases, but I think we fought a war in heaven for the privilege of coming to a place that was unjust. That was the idea of coming to earth—that it was unjust, that there would be pain and grief and sorrow. As Eve so eloquently said, it is better that we should suffer. Now, her perspective may not be shared by all. But, I am persuaded that she had rare insight, more than her husband, into the necessity of pain, although none of us welcome it.

I remember one time thinking such thoughts, such grand thoughts, and realizing that I dealt as a therapist with many people who suffered far, far more pain than I ever suffered. I felt guilty at having been spared some of the pain that my friends had experienced. Shortly after this, I developed a toothache. I'm a great chicken—I hate pain at all times. An apocryphal story was

told of my mother who, as she took me to kindergarten, told the teacher I was very sensitive and, if I didn't behave, to hit the child next to me. Although that's not a true story, it truly represents my sentiments. I'll learn from others, although I don't want pain myself. So when I had this toothache, I thought, here is a golden opportunity to embrace this existential experience and to join in this pain—open myself to this pain and experience it. I told myself I was just going to sit in this pain and take it into myself and grow from it. That lasted forty-five minutes, at which time I called my dentist and said, "I want some pain medicine." The forty-five minutes it took between the time I took the medicine and the time the pain went away was the hardest part because I showed no moral stature; all I wanted was to get rid of that pain.

So I do not want you to think that I believe anything good about pain. I hate pain. I hate injustice. I hate loss. I hate all the things we all hate. None of us love those things. Nor, as I say, do I think God takes pleasure in the pain that comes to us. But, we came to a world where we are not protected from those things. I want to talk to you not in behalf of pain—heaven forbid—nor do I think that all pain is for the best. I'm certain that's not true. I'm certain pain destroys and embitters far more often than it ennobles. I'm sure injustice is destructive of good things in the world far more often than people rise above it. I'm certain that in this unjust, awful world, there are far more victims who do not profit from their experience than those who do. So I do not want you to think I'm saying that pain is good for you. Pain is terrible.

I want to talk rather about when pain unbidden and unwanted and unjustly comes—to you or to those that you love or to these eleven-year-old girls as they get along in their lives. I want to discuss how to encounter that pain in such a way that it does not destroy you, how to find profit in that awful and unrewarding experience. I want to share with you some stories, mostly not my own, although I'm in all of them, but the pain is mainly someone else's. Some of the pain is my own. All of it is real, and all of it taught me. What I want is not to lecture to you or to sermonize you, but to share with you some lessons I have learned through pain, my own and others', that are valuable to me and, in the end, to share with you what I think I have learned from those incremental experiences.

The first two stories were extraordinarily

instructive to me. They both came through opportunities I had as a stake president to give blessings. Often the Lord has taught me through blessings; as I've had my hands on someone's head, he's taught me things I did not know and sometimes didn't want to know. The first one was a case of a sister whom I'd known for years and who, in my judgment, had made some very poor life choices. She had married a handsome, charming young man who initially wasn't a member of the Church but joined the Church for her. She waited a year to marry him and then went to the temple. It was the last time he ever went to the temple. I knew he was a flake from the beginning. Out of my wisdom, it didn't surprise me that he soon returned to many of his pre-Church habits—most of the transgressions in the

book that you can think of and some that I might not have.

There was great pain for this woman. A good, good woman, she kept in the Church; she kept in the kingdom; she suffered enormous pain because her husband went back to gambling and drinking and other things that were unhappy and unwholesome. But, the greater pain came when her children, having these two models before them, began to follow him. He would say things like, "Well, you can go to church with your mother and sit through three hours of you know what, or you can come to the race-track with me, and we'll have good stuff to eat and drink and have a great time." It was a tough choice, and very often the children chose to go with him. They gradually seemed to adopt his lifestyle, values, and attitude toward the Church and toward

sacred things. Although the mother never wavered from her own faith and faithfulness and her commitment to her Heavenly Father, her family was slipping away from her.

As she asked me for a blessing to sustain her in what to do with this awful situation in which she found herself, my thoughts were, "Didn't you ask for this? You married a guy who really didn't have any depth to him and raised your kids too permissively. You should have fought harder to keep them in church rather than letting them run off to racetracks." I had all those judgments in my head. I laid my hands on her head, and the Lord told her of his love and his tender concern for her. He acknowledged that he had given her (and that she had volunteered for) a far, far harder task than he would have liked. (And, as he put in my

mind, a harder task than I had had. I have eight good kids, all of whom went through the temple. All would have been good if they had been orphans.) She, however, had signed up for hard children, for children who had rebellious spirits but who were valuable; for a hard husband who had a rebellious spirit but who was valuable. The Lord alluded to events in her life that I hadn't known about, but that she confirmed afterward: Twice Heavenly Father had given her the choice between life and death, whether to come home and be relieved of her responsibilities, which weren't going very well, or to stay to see if she could work them through. Twice on death's bed she had sent the messenger away and gone back to that hard task. She stayed with it.

I repented. I realized I was in the presence of one of the Lord's great, noble spirits,

one who had chosen not a safe place behind the lines pushing out the ordnance to the people in the front lines as I was doing, but somebody who chose to live out in the trenches where the Lord's work was being done, where there was risk, where you could be hurt, where you could lose, where you could be destroyed by your love. That was the way she had chosen to labor. Then I thought, "I am unworthy to lay my hands on her head; if our sexes were reversed, she should have had her hands on mine."

Now she is doing well; one of her sons finally went on a mission. He had a bishop who took hold of him and shook him and got him to go. He went to one of those missions where people line up to be baptized when you get off the plane. He had a wonderful mission; they all but made an icon of him. He had miracles under his hands. He

came back hotter than a firecracker for missions. He wouldn't leave alone his younger brother, who was planning on playing football in college instead of going on a mission, until he also went on a mission. The younger boy looked up to his brother; nobody could have turned that second kid around except his older brother. The younger went on a harder mission. He happened to have a language skill that he developed, and he turned out to be the best one at the language. He caught fire, he had spiritual experiences, and he came back red-hot.

Those two boys started working with their sisters, who are harder cases; they haven't come all the way around yet. One of them looks better. One of them married a nonmember, and her husband did a terrible thing—he met the missionaries and joined

the Church and started putting pressure on his wife to become active. She said, "I married you because you were out of the Church." I don't know—even Dad may repent, who knows? She may yet win them all.

I do know that she risked her life for service. In a blessing, the Lord said to her, "When you're in my employ, the wages are from me, not from those you serve."

In the second case I had a woman come to me who was an incest victim—the victim of a terrible family. She was abused physically. Her mother was neurotic and stayed in bed all the time to get her daughter to do all the work, including taking care of the husband's needs when he was drunk. The daughter had been abused in about every way there was to be abused—psychologically, physically, sexually. Besides that, she had to do all the housework.

She was not a member of the Church at that time, although this happens to members of the Church also. In high school she met a young man who was a Latter-day Saint and who started taking her to church with him. Eventually they married. He was gentle and kind and patient because she didn't come with very many positive attitudes toward men, marital intimacy, or many other things. But he was long-suffering and patient and loved her. They raised some boys.

Despite this, she had recurring bouts of depression and very negative feelings about herself because she had been taught by the people most important in her early life what a rotten person she was. It was hard for her to overcome that self-image. I worked with her to try to build her self-image. One day she said to me, "You're a stake president; you

explain to me the justice of it." She said, "I go to church, and I can hardly stand it. When I see little girls being hugged and kissed and taken to church and appropriately loved by their fathers and mothers, I just have to get up and leave. I say, 'Heavenly Father, what was so terrible about me that, when I was that age, I didn't get any of that? What did that little girl do in the premortal existence that I didn't do so she is loved, so she is safe? Her daddy gives her priesthood blessings when she's sick. Her mother loves her and supports her and teaches her. What did I do?' Can you tell me that God is just if he sends that little girl to that family and me to my family?" She said, "It's a good thing I had boys. I don't think I could have stood to raise girls and have their father love them because I'm so envious."

I would not have known how to answer

her in my own capacity because her situation *is* manifestly unjust. Where, here or in eternity, is the justice in an innocent child's suffering in that way? But the Lord inspired me to tell her, and I believe with all my heart that it applies to many in the kingdom, that she was a valiant, Christlike spirit who volunteered (with, I told her, perhaps too much spiritual pride) to come to earth and suffer innocently to purify a lineage. She had volunteered to absorb the poisoning of sin, anger, anguish, and violence, to take it into herself and not to pass it on; to purify a lineage so that downstream from her it ran pure and clean, full of love and the Spirit of the Lord and self-worth. I believed truly that her calling was to be a savior on Mount Zion: that is, to be Savior-like, like the Savior to suffer innocently that others might not suffer. She voluntarily took

The Lord inspired me to tell her, and I believe with all my heart that it applies to many in the kingdom, that she was a valiant, Christlike spirit who volunteered to come to earth and suffer innocently to purify a lineage.

such a task with the promise that she would not be left alone and abandoned, but that he would send one to take her by the hand and be her companion out into the light. I viewed that woman in a different way also, again realizing I was in the presence of one of the great ones and unworthy to have my hands on her head.

I think we do not understand the nature of ourselves. I think we do not understand who we are. Some people call the temple ordinances the "mysteries" of the kingdom. When I went to the temple, I thought I was going to learn which star was Kolob, where the Ten Tribes were, and other such information. But those aren't the mysteries of the kingdom; the mysteries of the kingdom are who we are, and who God is, and what our relationship to him is. Those are the mysteries of the kingdom. You can tell somebody in plain English, but they still don't know in their hearts who they really are.

I was in a foreign country giving a workshop for others in my profession. The workshop was over, and I was just exhausted. My plane back to the States was to leave at 7:30 P.M., and it was now 4:00 P.M. I was right across the street from the airport in a motel. I thought, "This is nap time. I am going, in the middle of the day with the sun out, to take a nap." So I called the desk and said, "I want to be awakened at 6:00, not 6:00 in the morning but 6:00 in the evening; I'm taking a nap." I put down the receiver, undressed, and curled into bed and thought how deliciously wicked it was to be sleeping in the middle of the day. I had just snuggled down when the telephone rang. It was the mission president, who also was a General

Authority whom I had never met, but who had read in the paper that I was there. He had a problem with one of his sister missionaries. Although he'd been working with her, she had a ticket to go home on the same flight I was on. He'd labored with her and given her blessings. She'd been out only six weeks, but she was going home and nothing he was able to say changed her mind. The mission president said, "She said she had your text in college, and I told her you were here. I asked her if she would see you, and she said she would." He said, "You're it."

I protested, "It's your job; it's not my job. You're a General Authority—I'm just a stake president and out of my territory at that."

He said to me, "We'll send the car for you."

This sister and I sat down together. She

had her purse clutched and her ticket prominently displayed on it. She looked at me a bit defiantly, and I said, "The president tells me you're headed for home."

She answered, "Yes, and you can't talk me out of it either."

I said, "Why?"

She told me why.

It was an awful story. She had grown up in a Mormon family in Idaho—a farm family, a rural, poor family. She had been sexually abused, not just by her father, but by all her male relatives. She was terribly abused. Incidentally, I want to tell those of you who teach girls this, she had tried to tell a couple of times, and people wouldn't believe her. When she was ten years old, they had a lesson in Sunday School on honoring your father and mother. After class was over, she said to her teacher, "But, what if your father or your mother wants to do something that isn't right?"

The teacher said, "Oh, my dear, that would never happen. Your father and your mother would never want anything that wasn't right for you."

Finally, when she was fourteen, her Mia Maid teacher believed her and convinced the bishop it was so. The bishop took her out of that home into his own home, where she finished her high school years; he sent her to college, and then she went on a mission. Her father's "patriarchal blessing" when she left his home was this: "Well, aren't we fine folk now? Gonna go live with the bishop and all those holy joes over on the other side of town. Well, let me just tell you something, girl, and don't you never forget it. They can't make a silk purse out of a sow's ear."

That's what she decided on her mission.
She decided she didn't belong there with all
those silk purses. She was having sexual
feelings for the missionaries because when
you're only four or five when you first get
exposed to regular sex, it isn't easy. You
don't have the adult's or the teenager's sense
of proportion and sense of reality and sense
of the world to put it into proportion. So
here were all these attractive young men,
and she'd never had the opportunity to
develop in her life the kinds of protections
in her heart and in her mind that other
people in more blessed and protected circumstances have. She was having feelings
that she believed were unworthy and told
herself, "My daddy was right. You can take
a girl out of a family and send her to college,
you can send her on a mission, but you can't
change what she is—a sow's ear."

So she was going home to throw herself away because she didn't belong out here pretending to be someone she wasn't. I said to her, "Before you came on your mission, you went to the temple, didn't you? You were anointed to become a queen, weren't you, a princess in your Heavenly Father's house? That's no way to treat a princess. There may be—I can't imagine it—but there may be some justification in their backgrounds for the way those men treated you when you were young. I don't know; I can't imagine any. But I'm confident of this: The Lord will not easily forgive you if you treat his daughter that way. You're going to throw her away, a princess of our Heavenly Father? Then what are you going to say to him when he says, 'How have you handled the stewardship that I gave you of this glorious personage who lived with me, who is

my daughter, who is a royal personage of dignity and of honor? I sent her down to the earth, and how have you brought her back to me?'" She with the eloquence of her age and circumstances started to cry, but she stayed.

I saw her in Provo two or three years later when I was there speaking. She asked if I remembered her, and I did, which was a miracle in its own right because I forget my own children's names; I can't get them all straight. I remembered her and her name and said, "How are you doing?"

She answered, "I'm growing just as fast as I can. I thought you'd want to know." She understood who she was. I told her that I felt her stewardship was to get that daughter of our Heavenly Father home, home to Heavenly Father, home where she belonged. That's the mystery of the kingdom, that's the

mystery of godliness—that we are our Father's children.

Now I'm going to tell you three other stories. One of them concerns a sister I used to home teach years ago. She was something. Back then, the president of the Quorum of the Twelve was the one who sent out the schedules specifying when stakes would hold their conferences. For several years in a row we always had our stake conference on Mother's Day. It was nice because we saved money on carnations, but this lady was outraged. She couldn't see why it always had to be our stake on Mother's Day. She wanted the carnations and the respect for women. So she finally wrote a stern letter to the president of the Twelve, calling him to repentance for not observing the importance of motherhood. She said the priesthood leaders talked a good fight, but

That's the mystery of the kingdom, that's the mystery of godliness—that we are our Father's children.

where were they when it really counted on Mother's Day? And he changed the date of our stake conference. So you get some feel for this woman—a good woman, but not shy.

Anyway, I was her home teacher and her stake president. She was also one of those sisters who felt that if you just have a cold, it's all right to have your husband give you a blessing, but if it's anything more serious, you need at least the bishop. Stake presidents are better. If there's a General Authority in the area, that's the best. She wanted real sparks—none of this homegrown stuff.

They had two or three girls, and she'd had troubles with her deliveries, which were cesarean. Her doctor told her that she had nearly died the last time. He said, "Your uterus is so thin that when I was working there, I could see my hand through it. It is

not going to sustain another pregnancy. If you want to die, get pregnant again. Is that very clear? Will you let me take it out?"

She said, "No."

He said, "It's no good except to kill you."

She said, "Don't take it."

So he said, "All right, but I want you to know that if you have another pregnancy, you're dead."

Well, that lasted about four years. I accused her of having gone to see *Saturday's Warrior* one time too many. She decided they had a little boy up there waiting to come to their family. Her husband said, "Oh, no, you don't. You think you're going to get pregnant and leave me to raise those girls without you. No way; I'm not going to do that. The doctor told you, and that's sensible, and that's it."

"But I just feel there's still one up there for us."

"No way. We are not going to take any risks with your life. I'm not up to raising three daughters alone. I'm sorry; 'no' is the answer."

"Well, when President Broderick comes, let's have him give me a blessing."

Well, he got to me first, of course, and I couldn't have agreed with him more. I didn't want that on my hands. That's what we have doctors for. So I was not very moved by this woman's ambition to have one more child and said, "Now look, Sister so-and-so, you can't do this." But this lady is not an easy person to say no to. So her husband and I laid our hands on her head, and I heard myself telling this lady, Sure, go right ahead and have a baby. No problem. You'll have no problem in the pregnancy; it'll be just fine.

You'll have a fine big boy, nurse him, and everything will just be terrific. I could not believe I was saying it. Her husband was looking at me in horror. I left immediately.

But it happened just like the blessing said. It was just one of those stories where the Lord gives you the answer. She got pregnant. The doctor shook his head, but when the baby was delivered, it was fine. The uterus was fine; the baby was terrific. One little hitch—only it wasn't a little hitch; it was a big hitch. In the hospital somehow she contracted a blood disease, Haverman's disease. I'd never heard of it before, and I've not heard of it since, but it's vividly etched in my memory. She broke out in spots all over. They're very irritable, like having the skin scraped off your hand or off your back. She had at one point two hundred spots all over her body. She couldn't lie down or sit

down or be comfortable anywhere, and they looked awful. It looked as though she ought to wear a veil to cover these big, red, size-of-a-fifty-cent-piece blotches all over her body. There was a medication she could take to relieve the symptoms. Although it doesn't cure the disease, it does make the symptoms go away and allows you to live and function normally. But she wouldn't be able to nurse her baby if she took it.

"You promised in the blessing," she said, "that I could nurse this baby."

I said, "It was a throwaway line. What are you talking about?"

She said, "You promised, the Lord promised I could nurse this baby. I can't nurse him and take medication so you have to do something about this."

I said, "Look, get a bottle. Your husband can get up in the middle of the night. It'll be

terrific. Take the medication; you're home free—the baby's fine. Rejoice, you've got a beautiful boy."

She would not have any of that. She wanted another blessing to take away this disease so she could nurse her baby. I wished I were not her home teacher, not her stake president. But I put my hands on her head, and I heard myself telling her that her disease would go away and she would be able to nurse her baby. Then I left for New York—not just because of that. I had a meeting in New York, but I was glad not to be there hour by hour to see how it worked out.

I gave the blessing on a Sunday evening. Wednesday at two o'clock in the morning, I got a telephone call while I was in a deep sleep. I was president of this national organization and worrying about the next night

when I was to give my presidential address. It was hard to sleep, but I was doing my best. The call woke me, and she said, "You promised me these spots would go away, but they're worse. I visited the doctor today, and he says they're worse. Nothing's going well. You promised. I've done everything I know to do. I've been on the telephone all day to people that I might have offended, even in my childhood. 'Please, please, if there's anything I've done to offend you, please forgive me.' I'm trying to think of anything I've ever done in my life and to set it right. But my spots haven't gone away. Why?"

"I don't have any idea why," I said.

She retorted, "Well, don't you think you ought to have an idea? You gave me that blessing."

I felt terrible. I did something I've never

done before or since—I stayed up the rest of the night, what there was of it, praying. I said, "Lord, this woman's faith hangs on the blessing she received at my hands. I felt your Spirit at the time. If I was wrong, don't penalize her. Cover me." (And I started thinking of the people I should be calling.)

But she didn't call again, and I thought, *Maybe it's all right.* I got home Saturday night late, flying all day from New York, exhausted from the trip. I walked into the house, and there was a note that said, "No matter what time you arrive, call Sister so-and-so." I didn't dare not do it, so I phoned her. She said, "You get on over here." Is that any way to talk to a stake president?

It was two o'clock in the morning, but I went over. She was bitter and empty. She said, "I want you to know that I have no faith left. I felt the Spirit of the Lord, the

same Spirit when you gave me that blessing, that I've felt in sacrament meetings, in testimony meetings, when I read the scriptures, and in prayer. I felt that same Spirit, and here's my testimony." She raised her hands, which were covered with spots. "Well," she said, "what have you got to say?"

"Nothing."

"Don't you think you owe me an explanation?"

I said, "I have no explanation. I prayed all night. I don't have any idea why. I feel awful that I've been the instrument of your loss of faith. I cannot think of a worse thing that could have happened, that I could have spent my priesthood on, than to destroy your faith."

"Don't you think you owe me an explanation?"

"I tell you I have no explanation."

"You and the Lord—don't you think you owe me an explanation?"

"I'm not giving you any more blessings."

She said, "I think you owe me that, don't you?"

I never did anything with less grace in my life than when I laid my hands on her head. The Lord spoke to her, not of her disease and not of nursing babies, but of his love for her—that she was his daughter, that he cared for her, that he had died for her. He said that he would have died if she had been the only one. He would have suffered at Calvary for her sins, if hers had been the only ones. He didn't say one word about healing her.

The next day was fast Sunday. She came to church although she had said she never would again. With the spots she looked awful. It was not easy; she was not an overly

43

The Lord spoke to her
of his love for her——that she
was his daughter, that he cared
for her, that he had died for her.
He said that he would have died
if she had been the only one.
He would have suffered at
Calvary for her sins, if hers
had been the only ones.

proud woman, but it was not easy for her to appear in public looking as she did. She got up in testimony meeting, and her spots were worse than ever. She told the story and at the end she said, "I do not know why I have these spots, why my breasts have dried, but I do know this." And she bore a powerful witness of the Savior's love for her. That afternoon the spots went away and the milk came in, but not until she understood the mysteries of the kingdom, which don't have much to do with spots or milk or even with blessings, but have a lot to do with who we are and who our Father is, who our Savior is, and the relationship among the three of us.

I'm going to tell just two more stories. My mother, I trust, did not have a typical Mormon woman's life. She married three times, but she got better at it as she went

along. I've been grateful to her that she didn't stop until she got a good man. He wasn't a member of the Church when she married him, but he did join the Church and eventually became a bishop—a very good man. I'm sealed to him, and I love him. I wear his ring. He wanted me to have it because in his family when somebody died, people quarreled over the teacups. He wanted me before he died to have the ring so no one would quarrel over it, and I could have it. I wear it with love.

He died, in some ways, in a bad way, a hard way. He was a strong man—a man who'd been a sickly youth, but he'd done some of the Charles Atlas exercises. I used to love to hear him tell about how eventually he'd turned the table on the bullies. I was one who always ran away from bullies, walked to the other side of the street and

went home the other way, but I loved to hear his stories about how he'd finally gotten strong enough to take them on and beat them at their own game. I had a lot of vicarious satisfaction from his stories.

But at the end his lungs filled up with fiber so he had only five percent of his lungs to breathe with. With only five percent of the oxygen that he needed to metabolize his food, he just got weaker and weaker. His bones showed everywhere on his body. This big, beefy, all-solid-muscle man got to the point where all of his muscle had been eaten alive. I could easily carry him in my arms, although I'm not a strong man physically. He became petulant and childish because he could hardly breathe. He was constantly asphyxiated. He could hardly eat or go to the bathroom because he didn't have the oxygen to close his mouth that long. What

a strain to see this strong, good man waste away.

A week before he died I asked him for a father's blessing. He could reach over only one hand because he couldn't find a position where he could breathe and get both hands together. With that one hand, he gave me a father's blessing, which I treasure; I'd never had one in my life before. Then I asked him—and it was more talking than he had done for a long time in one space—I asked, "Vic, what have you learned from this six months of wasting away?"

He said, "Patience; I was never patient. The Lord has taught me patience. I wanted to die six months ago, and he left me. I've had to wait upon him. You know those stories I used to tell?"

"Yes, the ones I liked so well."

"Son, those aren't good stories; they're

full of revenge. They're not loving stories. I repent of them."

That man did not waste those six months. How many of us would have gotten bitter at God? "Why don't you take me? I've done everything; all I want to do is come home." That man spent those months being refined. I know he's presiding today over his family. We've done genealogy for his fore-bears and sent them up to him to work on in the spirit world. I know he presides over them today, and I know he's a better presi-dent of his familial branch in the spirit world than he was a bishop, and he was a good bishop. But, I know he was refined by his pain, by his adversity. He needed to go through that suffering. He could have been embittered; he could have been destroyed. His faith could have soured him and left him empty, but he chose to learn from his

pain. I do not want you to think that it was the pain that was good. It was the man that was good and that made the pain work for him, as indeed our Savior did.

One Easter a friend, after having brought two boys, then ages four and two, into the world, had a baby daughter. While she was in the hospital, her husband wanted to come to see the baby, but he had those little children at home. So his home teacher was kind enough to say, "Hey, bring the kids over. We've got a bunch of kids at our house. Bring the two kids over; my wife'll watch them." (That's not quite what King Benjamin said about service, but it's one step off.) "You go and see your baby."

So he did. While he was in the hospital seeing his new baby, his two-year-old got away from that woman's care and drowned in the pool. Through CPR she was able to

bring him back to his heart beating and his lungs working but never to real functioning. For two months he lay in a hospital bed, breathing, with his heart beating on machines that helped. His little knees some-how (I don't understand the mechanics of this) bent backwards. His feet bent back-wards. I don't know why. In the rigidity of his coma he became deformed. He had been a perfectly whole, wonderful child, but now it was hard for me to go visit him. I would go and sit beside him, looking at his mother who was rubbing him and singing to him. It was hard.

The ward fasted every Sunday for a month for that child. The members kept a twenty-four-hour vigil so that there'd be somebody he knew there when their faith made him whole. He was blessed by the stake patriarch, by the stake president, by a

visiting General Authority who was kind enough to add that additional duty to his busy schedule. In all those blessings the mother took hope. I will not say that she was promised flatly, but she took hope by what was said, that the child would live, that she would raise him in this life, and that he would perform many gracious acts and achievements. She would not even tolerate anyone's raising the possibility that he would not get better because she felt that everyone's faith had to be whole and focused.

I never saw so many people at the hospital—dozens of people kept vigil, fasted, and prayed for this child. After two months it became clear the child was wasting away and was not going to get better. His mother was the last to finally acknowledge what everyone else had come to see—he was not

going to live. It was costing, I forget how many thousands of dollars a day. So they finally decided to do the gracious thing and let him return to his Father. It was the hardest thing they ever did. They prayed, fasted, consulted with priesthood leaders, and finally, finally, decided the only thing to do was to pull the tubes. His mother said, "I can't stand it. I don't want to kill that little boy again. How many times is he going to die?"

So his grandmother went and held him in her arms when they pulled the tubes, but he didn't die. He lived another two weeks. I cannot express to you how spiritually exhausted everybody was when he finally died. The family had spent days and nights for weeks with him. Everybody had scarcely slept in two and a half months.

Just a week before that child died, the

newborn got a temperature of 105 and was taken to the hospital and diagnosed with spinal meningitis. It was a misdiagnosis, but they put the baby in the room just right down from the other little boy.

Her husband said, "Honey, let me go bless the baby."

She said, "You get your priesthood hands off my baby." She didn't want God to take that baby too. She said, "God's got all the babies he wants. Why does he want my baby? God doesn't need him on a mission—don't tell me that." People are not always helpful with the things they say. "God needs him worse than I need him—don't tell me that. He's got billions of babies, and I only have one; I have one two-year-old. Don't tell me he has a mission that can't wait fifty or sixty years more on the other side. There's

lots of work for him here. We'll keep him busy."

At the graveside the grandmother gave the opening prayer, and the grandfather dedicated the grave. In a somewhat unusual choice, both the boy's parents spoke. Can you imagine that? What they said was this: "We trust our faith will never again be tried as it has on this occasion. The things we have faith in have come down to a short list, but that list is immovable. We do not have faith that God must do what we entreat him to do." Earlier she had cried out to God, "I asked for a fish, and I got a serpent. I asked for a loaf, and I got a rock. Is that what the scriptures promise?"

But after it was all over, at her little son's graveside, she was able to say, "I am content that God be God. I will not try to instruct him on his duties or on his obligations

toward me or toward any of his children. I know he lives and loves us, that he is God. He's not unmindful of us. We do not suffer out of his view. He does not inflict pain upon us, but he sustains us in our pain. I am his daughter; my son is also his son; we belong to him, and we are safe with him. I used to think we were safe from grief and pain here because of our faith. I know now that is not true, but we are safe in his love. We are protected in the most ultimate sense of all—we have a safe home forever. That is my witness."

And that is my witness to you, that God lives, and he does not live less though you have injustice and adversity and pain and unkindness and violence and betrayal. God is in his heaven. We chose to come to an unjust world and suffer. But God is God, and he loves us. His son died for us. There